Y1
Gift

OVERSIZE

EVANSTON PUBLIC LIBRARY

3 1192 01360 1974

D1544549

914.11 Thoms.I Oversize
Thomson, Iain R.
Scotland :

MAY 2 1 2007

DATE DUE

AUG 0 4 2007	
SEP 1 2 2007	

DEMCO, INC. 38-2931

914.11
Thoms. I
Oversize

Gift to the

EVANSTON · PUBLIC
LIBRARY

*A gift
from
William Tomes*

Gift Book

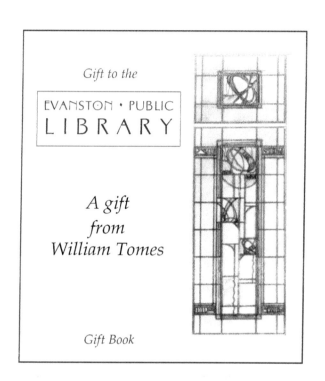

Scotland

A Photographic Journey

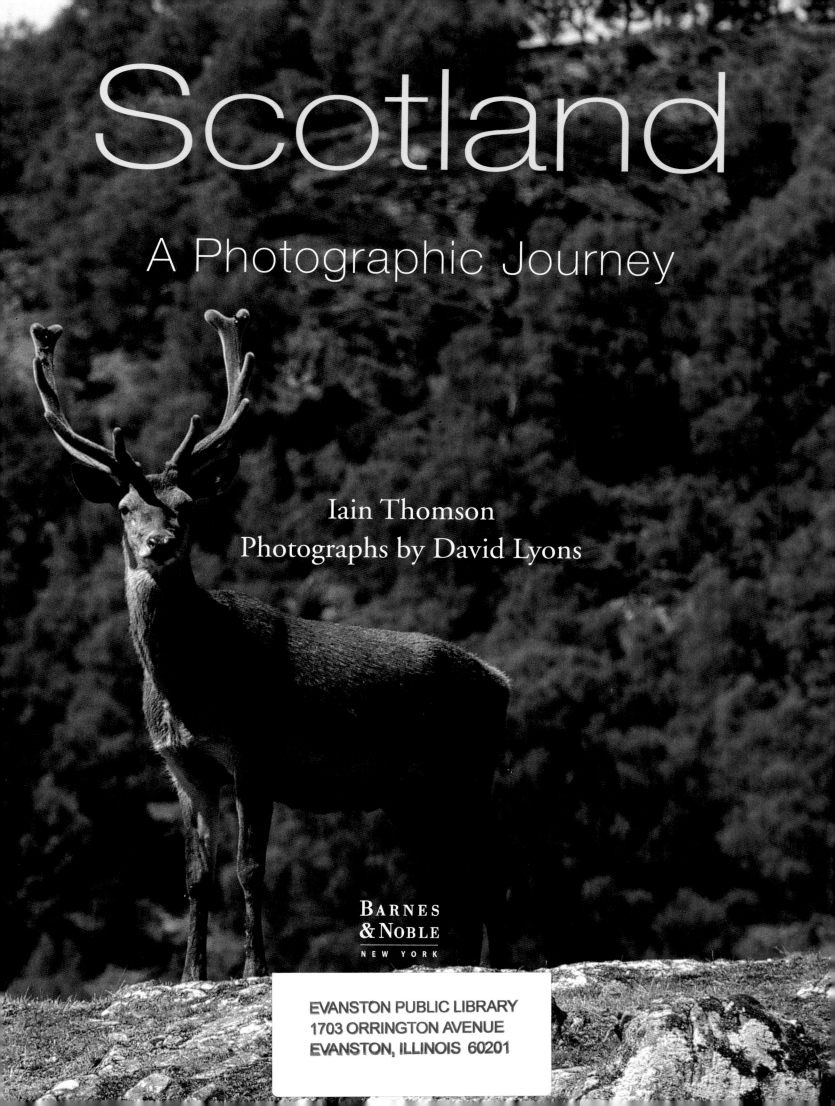

Scotland

A Photographic Journey

Iain Thomson

Photographs by David Lyons

BARNES
& NOBLE

NEW YORK

EVANSTON PUBLIC LIBRARY
1703 ORRINGTON AVENUE
EVANSTON, ILLINOIS 60201

This edition published by Barnes & Noble, Inc., by arrangement with Compendium Publishing Limited

2006 Barnes & Noble Books

Copyright © 2006 Compendium Publishing Limited

All rights reserved. No part of this publication may be reproduced, stored in a retrieval system, or transmitted in any form or by any means—electronic, mechanical, photocopying, recording, or otherwise—without prior permission of the publisher.

M 10 9 8 7 6 5 4 3 2 1

ISBN 0 7607 7338 6

Editor: Don Gulbrandsen
Design: Danny Gillespie/Compendium Design

Printed in China through Printworks Int. Ltd.

PAGE 1: Lichen on stone.

PAGES 2–3: The "Monarch of the Glen." Scotland's deer population has grown considerably in recent years—it has doubled since World War II. In particular the red deer—there are three types of deer in the country, red, roe, and sitka—numbers have trebled in the last fifty years to a point that some say that they are out of control and need culling.

RIGHT: Basalt columns near Fingal's Cave on the Isle of Staffa—these are from the same volcanic eruption that created the Devil's Causeway in Northern Ireland.

Contents

Introduction

Scotland is a beautiful country. All over the world there is a perception of the country gleaned from picture postcards and the lids of cookie tins—an image of bagpipes and whisky, deep brooding lochs and heather-clad glens, snow-capped mountains and salmon-fishing. Undoubtedly the Victorians had a lot to do with this. Paintings by such noted artists as Edwin Landseer, with his *Monarch of the Glen* depicting an imposing stag, and the romantic tales of Sir Walter Scott—allied to the queen's love of all things Scottish (including, it is said, her ghillie John Brown) have added to this image. From pen portraits to scenes of traditional Highland life, a rose-tinted picture of Scotland emerged that became enormously popular. It is really a foreigner's view of Scotland but it's also a view that has remained very potent.

The landscape of Scotland certainly includes its glens, lochs, and mountains but there is much, much more. The stark, rugged beauty of the Highlands contrasts vividly with the rolling moorlands of the Borders, with its vast forests and the majestic River Tweed. The shallow estuary of the Solway Firth and its sandy beaches, bordering England in the southwest of the country, could be a different country from the Atlantic storm-lashed wildness of the Western Isles further up the western seaboard. Anyone who has strolled along the "bonny banks" of Loch Lomond, been "over the sea to Skye," or has lingered in the beautiful woodlands of the upper reaches of the River Dee knows the allure of this country.

Undoubtedly the terrain and geographical features of the land would have shaped the lives and destinies of the Scots people—but who are these people? Why are they so different from their southern neighbors, and why are they so fiercely proud of their ancestry?

The Scots regard themselves today very much as one nation, but originally it was a country of many peoples. The northern islanders from Shetland and Orkney were of Norse origin, while the highlanders to the north and west of the mainland were Gaelic. The lowland Scot, on the other hand, was from Anglo-Saxon stock.

The turbulent history of Scotland reveals it to be a country of persistent conflict, almost constantly under siege but never fully conquered and on several occasions before the Union of the Crowns (of England and Scotland) in 1603, a state centered in the English lowland attempted to achieve the mastery of Britain. The incursion of the Gaels or Scots in the southwest brought them into frequent confrontation with the Picts, while in the Highlands there were the ceaseless feuds between the clans. At the beginning, and during the first half of the first millennium, the lowland people had to deal with the Romans; then, at the other end of the country toward the end of the millennium, the Northern and Western isles were invaded by Norsemen—the Vikings. The beginning of the second millennium saw the Normans conquer England and attempt to invade Scotland. Then within a couple of hundred years came the bloody feuds with the "auld enemy," the English. For more than 1,500 years Scotland hardly endured a decade of peace. Over the centuries, and during the course of these many bloody battles and conflicts, the peoples of Scotland, originally wary of each other, eventually began to accept themselves as one nation.

Early History

The history of the Scottish peoples begins in the Northern Isles—Shetland and the Orkneys—with the hunter-gatherers of the Mesolithic Age (around 7000 B.C.), through the Neolithic farmers (roughly 7000–2000 B.C.), the Bronze Age (2000–600 B.C.), to the Iron Age (600 B.C.–A.D. 500). It is almost certain that these people were Celts, although their exact origin is unknown. It is generally agreed that they were part of a minor stream of migrations from mainland Europe to the British Isles that took place in the first millennium B.C. and that it was a relatively peaceful colonization.

BELOW: The beach at Torrisdale Bay, Bettyhill, at the mouth of the River Naver.

LEFT: Pheasant: Scotland is famous for its country pursuits of hunting, shooting, and fishing.

What is also known—because it is readily apparent—is that the people in Scotland changed the landscape. Throughout the Northern and Western Isles there are many examples of stone circles built in the Bronze Age although their precise purpose remains unknown. There are splendid examples of these artifacts at Brodgar and Stennes in Orkney and Callanish in Lewis. One of the most important archaeological sites in Britain lies near the southern tip of Shetland. It was here, in the nineteenth century, that the Iron Age village, Jarlshof, was uncovered and it reveals the secrets and development of civilization from the earliest times through to the medieval age.

The beginning of the first millennium A.D. saw the Romans invade the British Isles and the attempted invasion of Scotland. After the Romans had mastered the southern portion of Britain, the Roman general Agricola crossed the Cheviot Hills (which lie along the modern border between England and Scotland) to complete the conquest of the island. Gnaeus Julius Agricola was responsible for much of the Roman conquest of Britain. He started his career started as a military tribune in Britain and later, as governor, he subdued Wales and northern England before invading Scotland. Starting in A.D. 79–80, Agricola consolidated Roman military control of the Forth–Clyde line and he masterminded building a string of forts across the country from west to east. He defeated the Caledonians, the last undefeated tribe in Scotland, at the Battle of Mons Graupius. Although the result was indecisive, Agricola's effort paved the way for the creation of the most northerly legionary fortress of the Roman Empire, at Intuthill in Perthshire. Agricola was recalled before he could finish his task of subduing Scotland. Perhaps because of this there is little evidence of Roman influence in the Highlands or Islands. It is entirely possible their

fleets sailed as far north as the Shetland Isles, but there is no proof of this. It is farther south, in the lowland plains and moors, that we find evidence of these southern European invaders.

With the failure to colonize Scotland, Rome adopted the alternative of maintaining a land frontier in the north.

Within the next few decades the Emperor Publius Aelius Hadrianus—we know him as Hadrian (A.D. 76–138)—visited Britain and sought to stabilize disaffected areas and protect the frontiers of his empire. A major portion of Hadrian's reign was spent on tours of inspection and his personal appearance among the border troops served to assure their loyalty. Up to this time all had not been well in Britain with many invasions from barbarian tribes outside the province. The forts constructed by Agricola in Scotland were so isolated that they were almost indefensible. Hadrian ordered the construction of his famous, eponymous wall as a deterrent to the raiding parties from lowland Scotland and the skirmishing tribes were contained behind the wall for more than 350 years. The great stone wall stretched across northern England from the mouth of the River Tyne in the east to the Solway Firth in the west, and became the frontier of the Roman province. Because of this Hadrian's name is written indelibly into the history of this evocative and diverse part of the United Kingdom.

In about A.D. 140 the Emperor Antoninus reoccupied southern Scotland and built forts and a wall of turf from the Forth to the Clyde to provide a "shock absorber" for Hadrian's Wall. The Caledonians twice destroyed the forts on the Antonine Wall and its defense was abandoned. The Caledonians continued to be a problem until they were subdued by the Emperor Severus, after which time the Picts took

ROBERT THE BRUCE

Robert the Bruce was probably born in Turnberry Castle on July 11, 1274. He supported William Wallace and became a Guardian of Scotland. In 1306 Robert declared himself King of Scotland and was crowned at Scone in March 1306. He launched his guerrilla warfare against Edward I gradually taking a number of Scottish castles and chivalrously allowing the defenders to return to England. During this time he issued the Declaration of Arbroath, often referred to as the Scottish Declaration of Independence:

"As long as a hundred of us remain alive, we will never on any condition be subjected to the lordship of the English, because it is not for glory or riches or honors that we fight, but for freedom alone, which no worthy man loses except with his life."

Bruce died at Cardross on July 7, 1329, and his body was buried in Dunfermline Abbey.

their place as the ruling people in central Scotland. In A.D. 367, with simultaneous attacks by Saxons from Germany in the east, and by Scots from Ireland in the west, the Picts overwhelmed Hadrian's Wall on the northern land border of the province.

In A.D. 400, three centuries after Hadrian's Wall had been constructed, Roman legions left the area. They were being recalled from all over the empire. Troubles at home meant they had to return to defend their homeland, and ultimately Rome herself, from the Goths. Within the next few decades not only Scotland, but also the entire British Isles, had been completely abandoned and Roman civilization began to unravel.

The Vikings

Nearly half a century after the departure of the Romans, towards the end of the first millennium A.D., a new danger threatened the Picts, Angles, Scots, and Britons as they strove for the supremacy of Britain—the Vikings.

Thanks to the Vikings' boat-building and navigational skills the Shetland Isles were a mere two days' sailing by longship from the fjords of the Norsemen's homeland. Orkney and the Shetlands provided secure bases for the Norsemen who settled there in great strength from about A.D. 800 onward. There were two currents of migration and settlement—first to Orkney, Caithness, and Sutherland; second, westward to the Hebrides, Isle of Man, and Ireland.

When the Vikings first arrived in Scotland they were only interested in conquest and plunder, but driven by the overpopulation of settlements on Norway's west coast, colonization of the ravaged territories soon followed. Far more than berserkers on the rampage, the Vikings were magnificent seafarers, explorers, traders, artists, and poets. Before long Norse society and culture had become firmly established in the Northern and Western isles, and the settlement of Vikings from Scandinavia would be one of Scotland's most formative influences. The language of the indigenous population, presumably part Pictish and part aboriginal, disappeared for centuries and a new language evolved. That this was deep-rooted is shown by the fact that a language descended from Old Norse was still being spoken in Shetland as late as the nineteenth century, more than 600 years after the Vikings had been defeated.

The Vikings lived next to and intermarried with the native Celtic populations and in the latter half of the ninth century a Viking jarldom (earldom) was established in Orkney. Throughout the settled lands jarldoms were established and, though semi-autonomous, each was under the ultimate sovereignty of the kings of Norway.

The Pictish society of Orkney and Shetland became almost totally submerged by the Norsemen and this continued unchanged until the thirteenth century when, following the Viking defeat at the Battle of Largs in 1263, Norway surrendered control of

BELOW: Landscape near Braemar on the River Dee. The Dee rises in the Cairngorms and flows for about 90 miles east to the North Sea at Aberdeen. The river has been called the "Silver Dee," a title it fully deserves with its tumbling, fast-flowing, crystal-clear water—so clear that it is often difficult to estimate its depth. Its headwaters flow turbulently in Highland glens set amid grouse moorlands until the main valley widens below Aboyne, where the river flows through well-farmed country. At intervals along its banks are enchanting woods of birch, fir, and pine that enrich the scenery and provide welcome shelter for fishermen. The pleasant scent of pine needles is a typical characteristic of the Dee as it pursues its rock course from pool to pool along its hill-enclosed valley. The valley of the River Dee has earned its title of Royal Deeside through more than a century and a half's connection with the British royal family.

LEFT: The Comet Stone and the Ring of Brodgar silhouetted against the evening sky. The ring—at Stenness on Mainland of the Orkney Isles—dates from the third millennium B.C.

MARY QUEEN OF SCOTS

Mary Stuart was born on December 8, 1542, and six days later she became Queen of Scotland. In 1548, at the age of six, her French mother sent her to the French court. At the age of sixteen she married Francis II of France and subsequently became Queen of France and Scotland. Based on the fact that she was the granddaughter of Mary Tudor, Mary tried to claim the English throne. To the Roman Catholics Mary's claim appeared stronger than that of Elizabeth—Ann Boleyn's daughter.

When the French king Francis died, Mary returned to Scotland where she knew little about the affairs of state and had neither the temperament nor training for rule. In 1565 she married a leading Catholic, Henry, Lord Darnley; like her, he was a great-grand-child of Henry VII of England. By marrying Darnley, Mary hoped to strengthen the Catholic cause and enhance her claim to the English throne. When Darnley was murdered in 1567, Mary was blamed and her rule was effectively over. Things got much worse for the tragic queen when she was implicated in a plot to assassinate Elizabeth I. She endured 19 years of captivity, first in Scotland and then in England, which ended only with her execution at Fotheringay on February 8, 1587.

BONNIE PRINCE CHARLIE

Charles Edward Stuart—also known as the Young Pretender or Bonnie Prince Charlie—was born in Rome in 1720. He was the grandson of deposed English King James II and the son of the Old Pretender James Stuart, who had twice tried unsuccessfully to invade Scotland to seize the English crown. After the disaster at Culloden, Bonnie Prince Charlie became a fugitive until, his alleged lover Flora MacDonald smuggled him to the Isle of Skye; from there he made his way safely to France. His supporters abandoned his cause and he died an alcoholic in 1788 in Rome.

RIGHT: The landscape east of Kinlochbervie near Achriesgill southwest of Durness. The fishing fleet from Kinlochbervie operated in the Northern Minch—the stretch of water between the Outer Hebrides and the Scottish mainland. Durness is the village closest to Cape Wrath, the northwestern extremity of Scotland.

the islands Kintyre, and Man to Scottish control. Norse control lasted longest in Shetland, which was ruled, directly from Bergen until the fifteenth century. In 1479, King Christian I of Denmark and Norway mortgaged the Shetlands to the Scottish Crown. Gradually over the next 150 years, Scottish law began to mix and combine with the older Norse traditions. Norwegian nobles, called "Lords of Norway" by the Shetlanders, continued to own large estates in the Shetlands, but were gradually ousted by the Scots by the sixteenth to seventeenth centuries. Still, the Shetlanders spoke Norse (or a variant thereof) until the eigthteenth century.

Today, the most enduring evidence of the Viking settlement of Scotland can be found in the many Norse place names throughout the northern isles, the Hebrides, and along the western seaboard. Shetlanders are still proud of their Viking heritage, celebrating it annually at the festival of Up-Helly-Aa, which resonates with Norse song, and is capped with a dramatic burning of a replica Viking ship by *guizers* costumed as Norse warriors.

Scottish resistance to the Vikings in this period was sporadic until Kenneth MacAlpin (mac = son of, so MacAlpin means son of Alpin), succeeded to the throne of the Picts. Born around the year A.D. 810, Kenneth's parents were from very different backgrounds, His father, Alpin Mac Eochaid, was king of Scottish Dalriada—but king in name only, as at that time Dalriada was ruled by the Picts. Kenneth's mother was a princess of the royal line of Picts. Kenneth was rightful heir to the throne of Dalriada on his father's side, but his mother's bloodline gave him the right to petition for the throne of the Picts—Caledonia. His opportunity arose in A.D. 839 when the Vikings and Danes waged a major offensive in Scotland in which "the flower of the Pictish nobility was destroyed." This attack allowed Kenneth to unify the remaining Scots and Pictish peoples, taking the throne in A.D. 841 as Kenneth I of the kingdom of Alba—later called Scotia. As King of Alba, he would change the face of politics in Scotland forever. He moved the capital from Dunndald to Scone, and in the process transferred the Stone of Destiny—on which the Pictish kings were crowned—to its new home. Scone became the place of coronation for most of the Scottish monarchs until coronations were move to England by Edward I in 1296.

The Tanist Period

Towards the end of the millennium the recovery of England from the Danes by Alfred (the Great) and his successors reached the north, when the Danes of Northumbria and the Norsemen of the coasts of Solway submitted to King Eadward. This brought Scots and Strathclyde Britons as well as Danes and Norse-

men together in a great coalition that was eventually defeated by Ethelstan, king of England. His successor subsequently destroyed Strathclyde and gave it to Malcolm I, King of the Scots, who thus became overlord of the Britons of Strathclyde including Cumberland. In 1005 the area we now call Scotland had three kingdoms—Alba in the north, Lothian in the southeast and Strathclyde in the southwest. Malcolm II, the King of Alba, brought these three kingdoms together when he conquered Lothian at the battle of Carham on Tweed in 1018. After Carham, much of present-day Scotland was under the control of Malcolm. Norse lords still held sway in Ross, Caithness, Sutherland, and the islands, while the men of Galloway remained fiercely independent. There was no doubt, however, that now the strongest power in northern Britain was the Scottish kingdom centered on the valleys of the Forth and Clyde. In 1034, Duncan, already ruler of Strathclyde, succeeded his grandfather Malcolm II as King of the Scots, thus uniting Strathclyde with Scotland.

Kingship in eleventh-century Scotland was not for the faint-hearted. Viking marauders still threatened from their base in the outer islands and Scottish politics was marked by internal strife punctuated by the all-too-frequent murder of kings and their potential heirs. The mayhem was largely due to an ancient practice of choosing Scottish kings called tanistry (or thanistry, as in thane). Under tanistry, succession was not strictly hereditary: rather, noblemen chose kings from a large pool of potential kings called tanists— any one of whom may have a legitimate claim to the throne through ancestry or marriage.

What often happened was the strongest and most cunning of the tanists would rise to power. As a result, the best person did not necessarily become king because tanistry encouraged open conflict as well as the assassination of reigning kings and other tanists.

MacBeth & Malcolm (Canmore)

When MacBeth murdered King Duncan I in Elgin, near Glamis Castle in 1040, it was generally seen as a good move. Duncan's rule in Scotland was no golden age and his six years of kingship brought glory neither to Scotland nor his family.

In contrast to the well-known Shakespeare character, King MacBeth's seventeen-year rule of Scotland between 1040-1057 was characterized by peace and tranquility and during his reign he united south and north and brought a semblance of law and order to Scotland. Unlike many other Scottish kings before him, MacBeth was so secure in his kingship that he was able to go on a pilgrimage to Rome in 1050 and return to reign for another seven years unchallenged, which was a remarkable achievement given the times.

BELOW: Much of Scotland's coastline is a haven for wildlife, in particular seals—the population is said to exceed 200,000. As with deer, there is a call for culling them, mainly from local fishermen who have seen populations spiral in the last fifty years. The colony on the Monarch Islands off North Uist, for example, leapt from 6,000 to 30,000 in the last thirty years and is estimated to eat over 75,000 tons of fish a year.

MacBeth was murdered in 1057 by Duncan's son, Malcolm, in revenge for his father's death. Malcom returned from exile in England with the intention of taking back the throne and this marked a turning point in Scottish history from which there was no looking back.

With the full support of the English, Malcom III (also known as "Big Head" or "Canmore") became the new King of Scotland, ruling until 1093. Under Malcom's reign, Scotland began the transformation from a Celtic to an English culture and Roman Catholicism began to have a major influence on Scottish politics. Because of Malcom's English ties, from then on the English would not leave Scotland alone.

The Expansion of England

The beginning of the second millennium saw the Norman invasion of England, which coincided with a time in Scottish history when the people were coming together as one nation for the first time. The border of England and Scotland at the time was very much like it is today. When Edward I, the "hammer of the Scots," came to the English throne at the end of the thirteenth century it marked the beginning of centuries of serious conflict between the "auld enemies." In 1286, Alexander III, the King of Scotland was killed in a riding accident. His three children were already dead, so his heir was his three-year-old granddaughter, the Maid of Norway. When she was six years old it was agreed that she should marry the eldest son of Edward I of England with Edward hoping this would eventually make his son king of England and Scotland. Edward's plans were thwarted however, when in 1290, the young Maid of Norway died while on her way to meet her future husband.

A great struggle for the throne of Scotland ensued when no less than thirteen people made a claim for the throne. The most powerful were the family of Bruce and the Balliols who claimed their right to the throne by saying they were direct descendants of David (1124-1153, son of Alexander I). It was submitted to Edward that he should make the choice and he chose John Balliol as the next king of Scotland. On St Andrew's Day 1292 King John was enthroned on the Stone of Scone (The Stone of Destiny). Edward's choice was widely criticized with general opinion being that Edward had really chosen little more than a puppet who he could easily manipulate. This fear was justified when Edward immediately began to undermine Balliol's power. He made a proclamation that anyone dissatisfied with decisions made by the Scottish king could appeal directly to him. Balliol, under pressure from his powerful lords, renounced his homage to Edward whereupon the furious English king demanded that Balliol should meet with him at Berwick—then Scotland's main

JAMES WATT

James Watt, born to a carpenter in Greenock, was one of the Industrial Revolution's most influential engineers and inventors. During his time at the University of Glasgow he met the chemist Joseph Black who, at the time, was studying the heat properties of steam. In 1769 Watt patented the condensing chamber for his steam engines and in 1774 went into business to produce these engines. The efficiency of Watt's engines made it possible for small industries such as cotton spinning to become large factory industries therefore helping to make the Industrial Revolution possible. Watt's legacy includes a laboratory being named after him at Glasgow University and, of course, the energy measurement, the "watt." James Watt died at Hatfield in 1819 at the age of 83 and was buried in Handsworth Church.

ABOVE: An old telephone box makes an unusual wood store.

ABOVE RIGHT: Scotland—in common with all the British Isles—is not immediately known for its culinary expertise, although standards have risen dramatically in recent decades. Kilmartin House near Crinan, Argyll.

trading center. When Balliol refused to meet Edward he massacred thousands of the townsfolk of Berwick and ordered that their bodies should be left to rot in the streets as a warning to others. Balliol immediately surrendered, but many Scots were unwilling to accept Edward as their king.

Edward invaded Scotland, but in 1297 the great Scottish hero William Wallace overthrew the English in a famous victory at Stirling Bridge where Scottish infantrymen were able to defeat a large English army of mounted knights.

William Wallace was born around the time Edward I—who was to become his deadliest adversary—succeeded to the throne of England. Wallace grew up to be a giant of a man, with a height of 6 feet, 7 inches, at a time when the average height of a man was little over 5 feet. Had Wallace not been a man of considerable strength and courage—and in possession of considerable fighting skills–he would not have become the hero of the nation that he eventually became. It was not only his physical attributes that made him such a hero, because his mental faculties were also considerable. As was the custom in those days the younger brothers of a family followed the education of the church while the eldest would inherit lands and titles. In those unsettled times it was prudent to have a firm grasp on languages and politics and the teachings of the powerful church. Wallace thus followed the career of a priest.

Wallace's father was killed in battle, which proved too much for a 19-year-old boy in a giant's body to

handle without taking action. He cast off the binds of the church and turned to his sword. He had grown up watching the cruel treatment of his oppressed country at the hands of the English and decided to strike back.

In 1296, Edward I of England invaded Scotland and the Scottish Wars of Independence began. Wallace began a guerrilla campaign against the English and became known as the hammer and scourge of the English. On September 11, 1297, the Scots defeated the English army at the Battle of Stirling Bridge. Rather than send their men two miles upstream to a wide ford across the River Forth the English elected to attack across Stirling Bridge. The bridge was so narrow it only permitted two men to advance at one time and, when a good number of English knights had crossed, Wallace attacked and cut a swath through the unprepared English. This attack cut the English army in two and reinforcements could not successfully be sent across the narrow bridge. The triumphant Scots could not believe the folly of the English. After the battle, William Wallace was knighted and put in sole command of the Scottish troops.

Wallace continued to create problems for the English until he was captured in 1305 and cruelly tortured and executed for treason.

Bannockburn and the Stewart Dynasty

It was now left to Robert the Bruce—a supporter of Wallace who declared himself king in 1306—to recover the Scottish kingdom. Bruce avoided pitched

ALEXANDER GRAHAM BELL

In 1847 the remarkable Scottish inventor and teacher, Alexander Graham Bell, was born in Edinburgh into a family with a passion for communication. In the mid-nineteenth century Edinburgh was brimming with scientific and technological developments. Alexander played the role of attentive observer and eager participant and with each passing year his intellectual horizons broadened. In the midst of his early academic and professional success, the young Alexander Graham Bell was battling tuberculosis, a disease rampant in Edinburgh, and at age 23, he moved with his parents to Canada to a spacious farmhouse in Brantford, Ontario.

In 1871, at the Boston School for Deaf Mutes, Bell began his revolutionary attempts to teach deaf children to speak. This led directly to his ideas about transmitting speech electrically and he read extensively on physics and devotedly attended lectures on science and technology. Drawing parallels between multiple messages and multiple notes in a musical chord, Bell arrived at his idea of the "harmonic telegraph." From this idea sprang the invention that made him immortal among inventors—the telephone.
after the conflict and was swept to power in 1932. As Taoiseach (prime minister) he brought in a new constitution, managed to maintain neutrality in World War II in spite of pressure from Britain and the United States, and became President of the Republic in 1959, remaining in that position until he retired in 1973. He died two years later.

battles and instead relied on guerilla warfare. After the death of Edward things went badly for England until only Stirling Castle was left in English control. Bruce's ultimate battle against Edward II, son of Edward I, is arguably the most important conflict ever to have taken place on Scottish soil. Bruce's stirring words: "Now's the time, and now's the hour, and Scotland shall be free" and the ensuing victory at "Blar Allt a Bhain-chnuie" or the Battle at the Burn of Bannock (June 23-24, 1314) was to win independence and assure Robert the Bruce the status of national hero.

Despite signing the Treaty of Edinburgh in 1328 that recognized Scottish independence and Bruce's right to be king, Edward III, like his father and grandfather before him, was determined to conquer Scotland. After Bruce's death the English king launched another attack on Scotland but the Scots' continued use of guerrilla tactics made it impossible for the English to subdue them. With the costs of war growing for the English taxpayer, Edward III eventually decided reluctantly to withdraw from Scotland.

In 1371 Robert the Steward, the first of the Stewart (Stuart) kings, succeeded to the throne of Scotland and so began a dynasty of 14 monarchs, five of which ruled both sides of the border. When they inherited the throne they inherited a land struggling to come to terms with emerging nationhood, but over the next four centuries they unified it. They brought the nation under central control and guided it through periods of renaissance, reformation, and

finally union with England. As we shall see later Stewart ambitions to regain the throne they had lost to their Hanoverian cousins were finally extinguished at Culloden in 1746.

The death of James V in 1542 left the throne to his infant daughter Mary Stuart, and from her reign the royal name "Stewart" took her spelling. The romantic figure of Mary Queen of Scots is, without question, the most renowned female in Scottish history.

The Union of the Crowns

It was during the reign of Mary Stuart that the new religion, Protestantism, took a grip in lowland Scotland, which in turn led to religious rivalries that would inevitably end in disaster. When Mary was forced to abdicate in favor of her son James it proved to be a momentous event in both Scottish and English history. In 1603, on the death of Elizabeth of England, James VI of Scotland was proclaimed James I of England, Scotland, France, and Ireland. He called his dual kingdoms of England and Scotland by a new name—Great Britain. With the Catholic, Protestant, and Presbyterian religions locked in an often violent struggle for supremacy, ruling the Scots from London was to be a almost-impossible task over the next century. When torn loyalties for the ousted King Charles II and his replacement William of Orange—regarded in the Highlands as a despicable "Englander"—were added to this volatile mix there were clearly many issues to fight about. Consequently seventeenth century Scotland saw the horrors of the massacre of Glencoe and the slaughter of the clans at Culloden.

At the beginning of the eighteenth century, in 1707, the Treaty of the Union, passed successively by the Scottish and English parliaments, received the royal assent and the Scottish Parliament ceased to exist. For many years the Union was bitterly unpopular in Scotland and in 1745 the Stuart dynasty made their last attempt to regain the throne of Britain—this dramatic adventure is known romantically in history as the "Forty-Five."

On July 22, 1745, Charles Edward Stuart—Bonnie Prince Charlie— accompanied by only seven followers, landed on the little island of Eriskay. The Stuart cause had to rely mainly on the Catholics of the northeast and the Highlands; the Presbyterian lowlands would not fight for the restoration of a Catholic king. To the English and the lowland Scots, who were increasingly becoming agricultural and industrial, the Highlands were virtually a foreign country. Nevertheless Prince Charlie, with a Highland army, occupied Edinburgh, defeated the Hanovarians at Prestonpans, and advanced towards London as far as Derby. If he had pushed on he may have succeeded in his quest, but with his support dwindling, on "Black Friday"—December 6—he made the decision to retreat and his dispirited troops faced the long march back to Scotland.

Meanwhile, the Duke of Cumberland, second son of George II, had built a formidable army at Aberdeen and six days later, to the surprise of the Jacobites (as the supporters of restoring the Stuarts to the throne were known) sheltering in Inverness, he arrived at the neighboring town of Nairn. The drums beat and the pipes sounded to assemble the Jacobite army and on the fateful day of April 16, 1746, the opposing armies met on the moor then called Drumrossie but now called Culloden. The disaster of Culloden extinguished the last hopes of the Stuart cause.

After Culloden

No place in Scottish history stirs the emotions more than Culloden. It had the dashing hero—Bonnie Prince Charlie—and the bloodthirsty villain—the brutal Duke of Cumberland. In the battle Charlie's Highlanders were outnumbered 5,000 against Cumberland's 9,000 and they were ill equipped and exhausted with poor artillery and few cavalry. They were destined to die in disproportionate numbers to Cumberland's men yet they went into battle with a courage that has passed into legend, and which today Scots the world over still salute.

By various acts of parliament the possession of weapons was forbidden and the wearing of Highland dress or of tartan became illegal. Later, the infamous "Highland Clearances" of the 19th century would finally see the end of the traditional Highland clan

ROBERT BURNS

With Robbie Burns, Scotland's favorite son, Scottish poetry reached its apogee. Burns was born on January 25, 1759, in the village of Alloway in Ayrshire. For much of his life he was a manual laborer and was well acquainted with poverty and deprivation. As a young man he started writing poetry, much of it in his native Scots language that was no longer regarded as the speech of "educated" men and women. Much has been written about "Rabbie" since his death but he undoubtedly had "an eye for the lassies" and much of his poetry is concerned with eating, drinking, and "wenching." He had the ability, unequalled among either Scottish or English poets, to write marvelous songs, exemplified by his amazing epic ballad Tam o' Shanter. Robert Burns was never a very healthy man and he died, aged 37, on July 21, 1796.

lifestyle. The history of the Scottish peoples in the 19th and 20th centuries was one of constant change as they took part in the revolution in agriculture followed by the industrial revolution. The destruction of the clan system, the prohibition of Highland dress and the extended knowledge of "English speech" gradually broke down the barrier that had separated the Highland Scot from the Lowland Scot.

The Scots took full and considerable part in the expansion, development, consolidation, and rule of the British Empire. Scotland had always produced more than its fair share of influential architects and engineers but has also been influential in the field of arts, particularly poetry, with a number of world famous writers.

Devolution

On September 11, 1997, 700 years to the day from William Wallace's victory over the English at the Battle of Stirling Bridge, a referendum took place in Scotland. The referendum asked whether Scotland should have its own Parliament. Nearly three quarters of the people who voted opted for creating a Scottish Parliament. Today, the Parliament is responsible for all Scottish matters but excludes "reserved" matters such as UK foreign policy, defense and national security and immigration.

Tourism is now Scotland's largest sustainable industry and it pays the wages of more workers than the oil, gas, and whisky industries combined. With the advent of the cheap airline seat tourists can get to Scotland on a very reasonable budget and the tourist industry is adapting to the short-vacation market that has been a large growth area over the past few years.

At the time of writing Scottish tourism is steaming ahead of the rest of the UK. Experts attribute Scotland's success to the country's transportation links and its ability to cash in on themed vacations, including golfing, mountain biking, and culture-oriented city visits. The country's tourist authority has worked hard to promote the country as a destination for long and short-vacation travelers and to encourage the millions of the Scottish diaspora to return "home." "Roots tourism" has become a major money-earner as the industry attempts to cash in on the history shared between Scottish descendants and the "old country." The history of this colorful country, though often bloody, is vibrant, lively, and never boring.

BELOW: View from Calton Hill toward Edinburgh Castle and Princes Street. The capital is a cosmopolitan city and hosts many famous festivals and events.

Lowlands

The most photogenic folly in Scotland, the Pineapple House was built in the eighteenth century by John Murray, Fourth Earl of Dunmore. It is 53 feet high, carved from stone, and is said to commemorate the first growing of a pineapple in a glasshouse in Scotland.

PAGE 21: Caerlaverock in Dumfries and Galloway, is a beautiful medieval moated castle. Triangular in plan, it was raised at the end of the thirteenth century and underwent many sieges—from that in 1300 by the "Hammer of the Scots" (King Edward I of England) to an altogether different siege in 1640 when it was held by Royalists.

OPPOSITE, ABOVE: Kelso Abbey was founded by King David I in 1128 and destroyed in Henry VIII's reign, in 1545.

OPPOSITE, BELOW: The Cistercian Melrose Abbey was another house founded by David I. It had been a monastery since the seventh century and—as with the other great foundations of the Borders—suffered badly during many wars until, as with Kelso, it was destroyed by the Earl of Hertford in 1545.

LEFT: Jedburgh Abbey was built on the site of a ninth century church and became an Augustinian abbey in 1147. Situated in the Borders it was regularly pillaged during fighting between the Scots and the English. This a detail of a romanesque doorway.

LEFT: A Border landscape—ruined homestead near Mervinslaw about four miles north of Carter Bar toward Jedburgh.

RIGHT: Last light on heather three miles southwest of Duns.

PAGE 26–27: View northeast from Carter Bar along the northern flank of the Cheviots into Scotland. The Southern Uplands is the southernmost of Scotland's three major geographical areas (the others being the Central Belt and the Highlands). The Uplands are a range of mountains and hills almost 125 miles long, stretching from Stranraer on the Irish Sea to East Lothian and the North Sea. Geographically they include the Cheviot Hills on the Scottish-English border, and the highest peaks are below 2,952 feet. Although the summits are not high in comparison with the Highlands, the area is remote and undulating. The Cheviots are the last range along England's Pennine Way, a 268-mile trail whose creation was inspired by the Appalachian Trail. The Way follows the high level Border Ridge—literally the England/Scotland boundary fence—for nearly 30 miles.

PAGE 28–29: Farmland near Ferniehirst south of Jedburgh.

LEFT: The bridge over the River Jed below Jedburgh Abbey has great strategic significance. Jedburgh lies on the main road from Newcastle to Edinburgh and its castle changed hands regularly until 1409 when it was demolished at the behest of the Scottish parliament—it is said that they were embarrassed by its regular occupation by the English

PAGE 32–33: Leaderfoot Rail Viaduct over the River Tweed near Melrose. Built in 1865 it has nineteen red sandstone arches. The River Tweed, in the Borders, is shallow and fast flowing, which makes it an ideal fishing river. The Tweed has its source in the Southern Uplands of Scotland. It appears at Tweed's Well in the west and flows in an easterly direction through Tweedsmuir, Peebles, and beyond. The river is 98 miles long and gains life from 1,500 square miles of watershed—the entire Borders region.

LEFT: Looking north to the Eildon Hills. The three peaks reach 1,327ft, 1,385ft, and 1,216ft—high for the area and, therefore, important land-marks.

PAGE 36–37: Heather on the Lammermuir Hills northwest of Longformacus.

RIGHT: Whithorn is one of the oldest Christian centers in Scotland—indeed, in Britain as a whole. Tradition has it that St. Ninian started his mission here as early as A.D. 397 and a Roman cemetery has been found on the site. This photograph shows a twelfth century doorway and the southwest corner of Whithorn Abbey.

PAGE 40–41: The delightfully named Sweetheart Abbey was a Cistercian house founded in the thirteenth century. Built from the distinctive red sandstone quarried at Caerlaverock, its name comes from the fact that the foundress—Devorgilla, Lady of Galloway—was buried in front of the altar along with the embalmed heart of her beloved husband, John Balliol, which had been her "sweet silent companion" following his death.

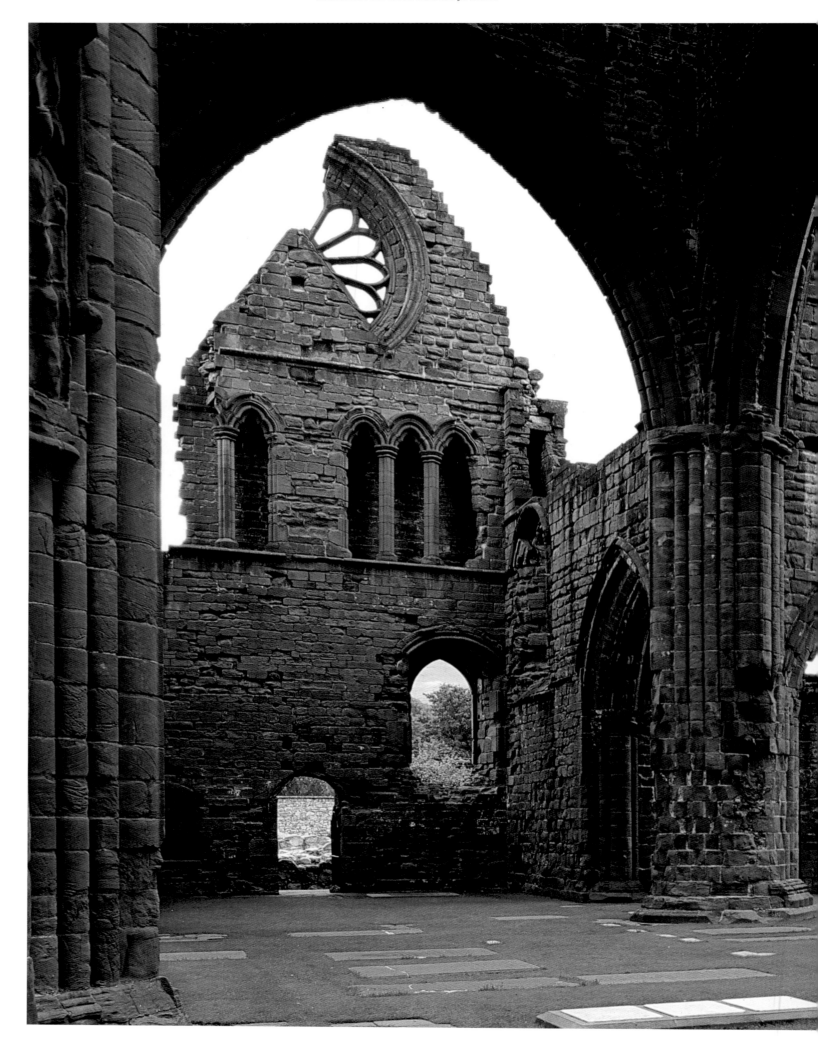

GOD·SAIF·YE·KIN
G·OF·GRIT·BRITAN·
FRANCE·AND·IRLAND
·OVR·SOVERAN·FOR·OF·
HIS·LIBERALITY·THIS·HO
VS·D I D·I·EDIFY

LEFT: House plaque beside Falkland Palace in Fife. Built by James III it was a favorite of the Stuart kings and it was here that James V is said to have delivered the melancholy prophecy of his death on hearing of the birth of his daughter Mary Queen of Scots: "It cam wi' a lass, it will gang wi' a lass." He was correct: he died shortly after.

BELOW LEFT: The texture of eroded sandstone in Kirkcaldy, on the north shore of the Firth of Forth.

RIGHT: Scott's view over the River Tweed to the Eildon Hills. Although primarily regarded as a Scottish river, the nineteen miles from Carham to Paxton mark the Scots border with England, and for its final four-mile journey to the North Sea from Paxton to Berwick-upon-Tweed the river flows entirely through England. The valley of the Tweed, and the region surrounding the river's many tributaries, is fertile land. The area is noted for its sheep and for the production of woolen and tweed cloth. Sir Walter Scott was born on August 15, 1771, the son of a lawyer. Scott's interest in the old Border tales and ballads had been awakened early in his life and he devoted much of his free time to the exploration of the Border country. He rose to fame as a poet and in 1805 was the most popular author of the day. Later he published several novels, including *Waverley*, which dealt with the rebellion of 1745. His last major poem, "The Lord of the Isles," was published in 1815, after which he traveled to France to collect material for his work on Napoleon. Scott died on September 21, 1832, and he was buried beside his ancestors in Dryburgh Abbey.

The Bass Rock and Tantallon Castle that juts out into the Firth of Forth atop 100ft cliffs. Scotland is fringed by many islands—one authority gives the number as 787. The Bass Rock is 350ft tall and has been home to hermits, a prison, and between 1691 and 1684 a fortress held by Jacobite officers after the battle of Killiecrankie.

RIGHT: The Thistle Chapel of St. Giles Cathedral. The Most Ancient and Most Noble Order of the Thistle is a chivalric order that was started in 1687 by James VII of Scotland (James II of England) and is today headed by the Queen. The chapel was added to St. Giles between 1909 and 1911. In fact, St. Giles is not a cathedral—the Church of Scotland has none—and only was one briefly in the seventeenth century. It is an old religious site, however: it has been the Civic Church of Edinburgh since 1120.

FAR RIGHT: Linlithgow is one of Scotland's four royal palaces (the others being Holyroodhouse, Falkland, and Scone). A royal residence since the twelfth century, Linlithgow Palace was started by James I and both James V and his daughter Mary Queen of Scots were born here.

PAGE 48:

TOP: Edinburgh—the Old Town by moonlight.

BELOW: Edinburgh's North Bridge crosses between Old and New Town. Designed by Robert Adam, construction lasted from 1763 to 1772. The Georgian New Town stated building in 1767. Adam also designed the South Bridge which was completed in 1788.

ABOVE: The Palace of Holyroodhouse in Edinburgh. The living heart of Scotland's history, Edinburgh (correctly pronounced ED-in-bu-ruh) is named after Edwin, King of Northumberland in the seventh century. It is Scotland's capital and second largest city. To the south of Holyroodhouse stands the dramatic landmark of Arthur's Seat, an 823-foot-high stump of an extinct volcano, from which a stunning panoramic view of the city can be seen. The name has nothing to do with England's fabled King Arthur, but is more likely associated with Prince Arthur, a sixth century Prince of Strathclyde.

LEFT: The John Knox Window commemorates the association of the great reformer with St. Giles. The Scottish Reformation started with a sermon by Knox on June 29, 1559, and he became Minister of St. Giles. His statue stands in the nave.

Edinburgh Castle from Princes Street gardens. At the west end of the Royal Mile, Edinburgh Castle, which dates from the twelfth century, stands proudly atop a dramatic outcrop of volcanic rock and overlooks the city's famous shopping avenue—Princes Street.

JOHN
KNOX
HOUSE

GOD·ABVFE·AL·AND·YI·NYCHTBOVR ⌒⌒ ∾ AS·YI·SELF

LEFT AND ABOVE: John Knox's house in Edinburgh on the Royal Mile. The backbone of Edinburgh's Old Town is the almost east–west axis of the Royal Mile that runs from Edinburgh Castle to the Palace of Holyroodhouse and the new Scottish Parliament Building. This main street is variously called Castle Hill, Lawnmarket, High Street, and Canongate. This street links the two landmarks that make Edinburgh a city in which it is almost impossible to get lost.

PAGE 54–55: The Firth of Forth is an estuary of the River Forth and an inlet of the North Sea. To the north of the firth is Fife; West Lothian, the City of Edinburgh, and East Lothian lie to the south. The River Forth is tidal as far inland as Stirling, but it is generally considered that the inland extent ends at the Kincardine Bridge. On the banks of the firth stand Edinburgh's main port, Leith, the Rosyth naval base, and the petrochemical complexes at Grangemouth and Burntisland. The firth is crossed by the Forth Rail Bridge, which opened in 1890, and the later Forth Road Bridge, which opened in 1964.

PAGE 56–57: Bass Rock bird sanctuary and light as seen from the ruins of Tantallon Castle. (See also pages 44–45.)

THIS PICTURE: Barns Ness lighthouse on the coast east of Dunbar.

LEFT: The administrative area of Strathclyde covers the west of Scotland from the Inner Hebridean islands of Mull, Coll, and Tiree to the south bank of the Firth of Clyde. The estuary of the River Clyde from its upper tidal limit in Glasgow city center, to the outer firth in Argyll and Ayrshire, forms the Firth of Clyde. The firth includes many sea lochs, peninsulas, and islands, with the islands of the lower Firth of Clyde being the smallest of the three major Scottish island groups, after the Hebrides and the Northern Isles (see pages 158 onward.). In Victorian times, with the advent of tourism, the area became popular with well-to-do Glaswegians who traveled "doon the water" on pleasure steamers to the picturesque seaside towns that line the firth. This photograph was taken on the Isle of Mull, looking across Loch na Keal toward the slopes of Ben More.

ABOVE LEFT: Glen Luss lies on the west side of Loch Lomond, northwest of Glasgow, in the Loch Lomond and the Trossachs National Park. In Scotland, the word loch is used to describe any large, enclosed expanse of water including areas coming in from the sea as in the Norwegian fjords. Much of Scotland's natural beauty derives from its many picturesque lochs and each of

these freshwater lakes has its own special charm—none more so than Loch Lomond. The loch is Scotland's largest and also the largest body of fresh water in Britain. It extends 24 miles north from Balloch to Ardlui. The loch is bordered on all sides by mountains and hills and its "bonny banks" are legendary, without a dull viewpoint throughout its length. At its wider southern end there are some 30 wooded islands, many of which were inhabited in the fifth century by Irish missionaries. St. Mirren is believed to have founded a monastery on Inchmurrin, the largest of these islands, in the sixth century. Another of the islands, Inccailloch, is owned by the Scottish Natural Heritage and is the burial place of the MacGregors and the MacFarlanes.

ABOVE: Inverary was constructed as a "new town" after being burned to the ground by the Earl of Montrose in 1644 during the civil war. On the banks of Loch Fyne, it was rebuilt in the mid-eighteenth century.

PAGE 62–63: Staffa is a small island off the west coast of Mull famous for its basalt columns and Fingal's Cave, immortalized by the composer Mendelssohn.

RIGHT, FAR RIGHT, AND BELOW:
Iona lies of the southwestern tip of
Mull—the Ross of Mull. An early
Christian site of great age—
St. Columba landed there in
A.D. 563 from Ireland to found a
monastery from whence
missionaries could bring the gospel
to the Picts—it had been an important druidic location before then.
The island once had 350 crosses, a
monastery, and a cathedral. The
Reformation destroyed this and it
was only in the twentieth century
that restoration began. Today, the
Cathedral Church of St. Mary
(BELOW) and a few of the Celtic
Christian crosses survive, including
that of St. Martin; the Cross of
St. John (FAR RIGHT) is a replica,
the original being housed in the
museum. The monastic cloisters
have been rebuilt (RIGHT).

FAR LEFT: The fifteenth-century Kilchurn Castle sits on a peninsula at the north end of Loch Awe.

LEFT AND PAGE 68–69: North of Loch Awe lies Loch Linnhe, which runs from the eastern edge of Mull to Fort William. The sixteenth-century Castle Stalker lies near the southern shore of Loch Linnhe near Port Appin.

LEFT: Glasgow—the Victorian Italian Renaissance-style entrance loggia to the city chambers. During the Industrial Revolution Glasgow built up a thriving textile industry. The city also became an important shipbuilding center, and by 1835 half the tonnage of steamships built in Britain was constructed on the Clyde—although the center of the city was not accessible to shipping until improvements were made to river navigation in the 1840s. The economy of the city also benefited from the development of the rail system that linked the main industrial centers of England to Glasgow.

ABOVE RIGHT: The Chinese Room in Glasgow's Burrell Art Collection. After Scotland's union with England in 1707 the city prospered, especially through the lucrative trade established with the New World. The port on the River Clyde began importing tobacco, sugar, cotton, and other goods from the Americas. A large percentage of these goods were then exported to continental Europe. Later trade expanded to take in the Far East as exemplified by the artworks shown here. Sir William Burrell (1861–1958)—whose family had made their money from shipping—gifted his art collection to Glasgow in 1944 and a gallery was finally opened in 1983.

RIGHT: St. Mungo's Cathedral. Glasgow, sitting on the mighty River Clyde, is Scotland's largest city and the administrative center of the Strathclyde Region. It is believed to have grown up round a Christian settlement established in the late sixth century by St. Mungo, whose church was probably on the site of the present cathedral.

Kilchoan megalithic tomb in Kilmartin Valley. There are many prehistoric remains in this area that point to a neolithic settlement of some size.

LEFT: Surface decoration from a beaker dating back to 3000 B.C. from the Nether Largie South burial chamber in Kilmartin Valley.

ABOVE: This food vessel dating back to the second millennium bc was retrieved from Glebe Cairn in Kilmartin Valley.

RIGHT: The portal and door from sixteenth-century Hornby Castle, Yorkshire, were incorporated into the gallery that houses the Burrell Art Collection.

PAGE 76–77: This photograph looks across the sound of Jura from the mainland to the island in stormy weather.

RIGHT: Dumbarton rock is a 240ft high plug of volcanic basalt. There has been a fortress here since the fifth century—although most of the buildings only date back to the seventeenth and eighteenth centuries.

PAGE 80–81: Arichonan is a deserted village near Lochgilphead, which stands at the head of the Crinan Canal. This runs from Crinan on the Sound of Jura to Loch Gilp on Loch Fyne—cutting the need for shipping to round Kintyre.

ABOVE: The island of Colonsay lies north of Islay. This photograph looks southwest over the Colonsay and Oronsay toward Islay.

RIGHT: Eas Fors waterfall on the Isle of Mull.

FAR RIGHT: The circular parish church in the village of Bowmore on Islay. The village was laid out in 1768 and the church was built in 1769.

RIGHT: North of the Firth of Forth, on the east of Scotland is the Firth of Tay situated between the regions of Fife and the City of Dundee and stretches for more than 20 miles. For much of its length the main channel of the estuary lies close to the southern shore and the most extensive intertidal flats are on the north side, west of Dundee. Monifieth Bay, to the east of Dundee, contains some extensive mussel beds, while the Inner Tay Estuary is noted for its reed beds. Birds abound in the area; in the summer the firth is important for breeding terns and marsh harriers, while in the winter and breeding seasons the estuary holds major concentrations of wading birds, sea ducks, and geese. One of the tributaries to the Tay is the River Garry which flows through the Pass of Killiecrankie just north of Pitlochry. It was at Killiecrankie on July 27, 1689, that James II's forces caught a Williamite army under Hugh Mackay and defeated it soundly.

PAGE 86–87

LEFT: The entrance to Brechin round tower. Brechin stands on the River Usk which flows into the North Sea at Montrose. The 87ft tall round tower dates back to the tenth or eleventh centuries—in appearance more like the Celtic towers in Ireland.

RIGHT: Detail of a seventeenth century carving of Death taking an old woman on Arbroath Abbey (see page 88).

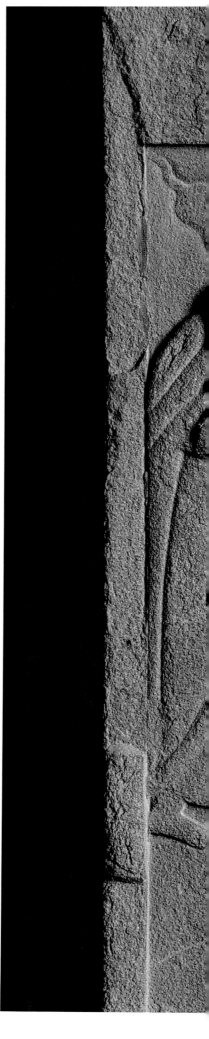

THIS PICTURE: Originally a Cluniac priory founded in 1178, Arbroath Abbey did not suffer at the Reformation but fell into disuse in the seventeenth century.

BELOW: There are ten standing stones in three groups on the eastern edge of Fortinghall village above the River Lyon. There's a legend that Pontius Pilate was born here—and his father certainly could have been a legionary on North Britain.

PAGE 89: The Tay is the longest river in Scotland and is one of the most prolific salmon rivers of the world. It stretches a distance of 120 miles from the northern slopes of Ben Lui to the Firth of Tay beyond Perth. The river has a variety of names on its 100-mile journey. It rises as the Fillan at the western end of Breadalbane and flows southeastward through Strath Fillan where it becomes the Dochart at Crianlarich. From there it continues eastward through Loch Dochart and Loch Iubhair in Glen Dochst to join Loch Tay at Killin. Issuing from the eastern end of Loch Tay, the River Tay proper flows east and southeast, cutting its way through dramatic scenery on its way to Perth before emptying into the Firth of Tay near its junction with the River Earn. Dundee is on the north bank of the firth and, two miles to the east, opposite Tayport, is Broughty Castle. This started life in the sixteenth century but was taken over by the War Department in 1855 and modified as a coastal fort.

RIGHT: Farmland near Blairgowrie: the area is well known for its raspberries and fruit.

PAGE 92–93: Blair Castle at Blair Atholl, the home of the dukes of Atholl. Started in the thirteenth century, it endured one of the last sieges of any castle in Britain when it was attacked by the Duke of Atholl after it had been taken by government troops during the 1745 rebellion. Today's castle is an eighteenth century reconstruction.

Highlands

PAGE 94–95: The hills above Loch Muick. The Highlands, north and west of the Highland Boundary Fault, are the mountainous regions of Scotland. The ranges are rough, beautiful, and magnificent places that attract many international visitors—but their slopes can have a darker side. Despite their modest height, walking and climbing in these mountains may be made treacherous because of their latitude and exposure to Atlantic weather systems. Even in summer, conditions can be atrocious, with thick fog, strong winds, driving rain, and freezing summit temperatures commonplace.

LEFT: A detail from the top of Union Street, Aberdeen. Scotland's third-largest city, Aberdeen, situated on the east coast, is the administrative center for Grampian and its largest fishing port. Aber is the Gaelic word for river mouth—so Aberdeen derives its name because it lies between the mouths of the rivers Dee and Don. The city developed from two separate settlements, Old Aberdeen around St. Machar's Cathedral in the north, and a more commercial settlement in the south around the harbor on the Dee. Aberdeen has been a port since Roman times, but by the end of the thirteenth century it was exporting fish, wool, and hides to other parts of Britain and Europe. Aberdeen is known as the "Granite City" because this local stone is used predominantly in its buildings. It is more romantically referred to as the "Silver City" after the effect caused when the sun comes out after rain. The shiny speckles of quartz in the granite glint in the sunlight, creating a dazzling spectacle, especially when the city is viewed from the surrounding hills. In more recent times Aberdeen has benefited hugely from the North Sea oil boom with the city becoming very prosperous.

LEFT: Sunset over Dunnottar Castle. Situated on the coast south of Aberdeen, Dunnottar started life in the twelfth century, but it was in the fourteenth that the Great Marischal of Scotland, William Keith, built a tower-house. Besieged in 1645 and 1651 during the Civil War, it was slighted after the 1715 Jacobite rising.

PAGE 100–101

ABOVE LEFT: Cullerlie standing stones date back to the second millennium B.C.

ABOVE RIGHT: Marischal College was founded in 1593 by the Fourth Earl Marischal and is now part of Aberdeen University. It is the second largest granite structure in the world (after the Escorial Palace in Madrid).

BELOW: Lochnagar rising above Loch Muick. The northeast corner of Scotland—from the Firth of Forth in the south to the Moray Firth in the north—is quintessentially Scottish. It is here that we find the Grampian mountain range, considered to be the separation between the Highlands and Lowlands of Scotland. They extend southwest to northeast between the Highland Boundary Fault and Glen Mor (the Great Glen), occupying almost half the land area of Scotland.

RIGHT AND BELOW: Angels playing bagpipes—details from Rosslyn Chapel (Below) and St. Giles Cathedral, Edinburgh (Above). When, in Scottish highland history, the bagpipes replaced the harp as a call to arms is uncertain. What is not uncertain is that a bard twanging away while singing an exhortation in the frosty dawn to hundreds of highland warriors—most of them, in all likelihood, out of earshot— offered nothing compared to the effect of the pipes shrieking through the misty glens. The courage of the pipers in battle, inevitably a lone target, has become legendary through the centuries and there are memorials all over Scotland to these brave souls. At the Haughs of Cromdale, near Grantown on Spey, there's the Piper's Stone onto which a badly wounded piper in the Jacobite army climbed and continued to play, although the battle was lost, until he died. In the border country the Piper's Pool is still remembered where an intrepid piper played, to rally Montrose's troops in 1645, until a bullet knocked him into the river, where he drowned.

FAR RIGHT: Pipe band at the Braemar Gathering. The sight and sound of the Highland regiments, in their kilts and with their pipers, who fought in World War I were so terrifying to the enemy in their opposing trenches that they earned the nickname "The Ladies from Hell."

RIGHT: Pictish stone detail from Shandwick on the north coast of the Moray Firth.

BELOW RIGHT: A memorial cairn on the battlefield of Culloden. Fought on April 16, 1746, it was a disaster for the 5,000 Highlanders that composed the Jacobite army. After a Jacobite night attack went wrong, the 9,000 government forces under "Butcher" Cumberland decimated Charles Stuart's Highlanders effectively ending the rebellion.

FAR RIGHT: The Caledonian Canal runs for 60 miles along the Great Glen from Cornach, near Fort William, in the southwest, to Inverness in the northeast. The Great Glen divides Scotland in half and was formed by a geological fault. This enormous fracture of the earth's crust left the fissures that are now filled by the waters of Loch Dochfour, Loch Lochy, Loch Oich, and Loch Ness. Officially, the Caledonian Canal is 60 miles long, but 38 miles traverse these famous lochs. The remaining 22 miles of actual canal include 29 locks. Just north of Fort William the canal negotiates Neptune's Staircase, an impressive engineering feat that raises vessels to a height of 70 feet above sea level through a ladder of eight locks. The canal was started in 1803, built according to plans produced by Thomas Telford. Once finished, in 1822, it provided the long-hoped-for route between eastern and western Scotland. It might seem strange to find a ship canal in the Scottish Highlands when they are normally associated with the great industrial cities, but the canal allowed mariners to avoid the often-hazardous sea route around the west coast of Scotland and through the perilous Pentland Firth. Inverness stands at head of the Moray Firth and at the entrance of the Caledonian Canal. The northernmost city in Scotland, it is often referred to as the "capital" of the Highlands.

LEFT: The early nineteenth-century
bridge built by Telford at Inver-
moriston on the west side of Loch
Ness. The 24-mile-long loch is
comparatively narrow but has great
depth. Of all the Scottish lochs this
one most resembles a Norwegian
fjord, with the surrounding hills
plunging at an angle of almost 45
degrees into its deep murky waters.
The great depth of the loch means
it never freezes over and even during
the coldest winters maintains an
almost constant temperature of
42°F. However unusual and sceni-
cally attractive Loch Ness may be,
what draws the visitors are the
legends and reports of its great
monster—Nessie. The current spate
of interest in this beast stems from
the 1930s but stories and sightings
go back into antiquity. The earliest
witness is alleged to have been St.
Columba in A.D. 565. There have
been frequent, alleged sightings of
the monster—but in spite of many
investigations no concrete evidence
of its existence has been found and
Nessie, if she exists, remains as elu-
sive as ever.

ABOVE: At the top of Glencoe stands the Buchaillie Etive Mor—the great shepherd of the glen—whose 3,345ft summit, Stop Dearg, affords fabulous views of Rannoch, the glen itself, and over the Aonach Eagach ridge the Mamores and Ben Nevis massif. Being over 3,000ft it is a "Munro"—Scotland's highest mountains are known as Munros, named after Sir Hugh Munro who, in 1891, surveyed all the country's mountains above 3,000 feet. All the Munros are in the Scottish Highlands and Western Islands.

LEFT: Rannoch Moor east of Glencoe is a bleak place—20sq miles of peat bogs and small lakes surrounded by mountains and traversed by the road from Crianlarich to Ballachulish that passes through Glencoe.

RIGHT: At Clava, southeast of Inverness, there are three neolithic tombs—the stone circles have been added later.

PAGE 110–111: An atmospheric view of thirteenth-century Eilean Donan Castle which stands on Loch Duich on the road to Kyle of Lochalsh.

RIGHT: At the head of tidal Loch Moidart on the north edge of the Ardnamurchan peninsula, thirteenth-century Tioram Castle is superbly located high on a rock islet. It was at the center of the two Jacobite risings of 1715 and 1745 and was slighted after the '45, although parts remained habitable.

PAGE 114–115: This view down Glencoe is punctuated on the left by Gearr Aonach, the middle of the Three Sisters of Glencoe (she is flanked by Beinn Fhada and Aonach Dubh).

PAGE 116–117: The head of Glencoe showing the classic U-shape of a glaciated valley.

LEFT: High on the northwest coast, just east of Cape Wrath, is Loch Eriboll, a deep-water loch that was used as a fleet anchorage in World War II and was where German U-boats were assembled after the surrender.

PAGES 120–121: Further east from Loch Eriboll, toward Bettyhill, Invernaver lies on Torrisdale Bay. There are many such ruined cottages in the Highlands, testament to the harsh realities of life in this area.

THIS PICTURE: West of Loch Eriboll is Durness, the closest village to Cape Wrath. This photograph looks northeast over the beach at Traigh na h Umamhag.

PAGE 124: Dunnet Head lighthouse on the Pentland Firth, the strait between the Scottish mainland and the Orkney Islands.

LEFT: Jerpoint Abbey is one of the most impressive ruins in Ireland. A Cistercian house founded in 1158, it became affiliated with another great Cistercian foundation—Fountains Abbey in Yorkshire—in 1227. The cloistered quadrangle is particularly evocative and it is from the cloister pillars that this detail of a bishop and a knight is taken

BELOW: Wolves are bred at the wildlife park at Kingussie. Legend has it that the last wolf in Britain was killed in the Highlands in 1743 by a character named MacQueen. As elsewhere in the world there have been moves to reintroduce the wolf to its old habitat, although local farmers are—understandably—reluctant.

PAGE 126–127: Sea fog shrouds the eroded stacks of Duncansby Head, east of John o'Groats.

THIS PICTURE: The Glennfinnan monument to the '45 rebellion was erected beside Loch Shiel in 1815. It commemorates the raising of the standard of Prince Charles Edward Stuart —"Bonnie Prince Charlie"— on August 19, 1745.

PAGE 130–131: A North Sea oil rig enters Cromarty Firth, on the northeast coast near Inverness. North Sea oil and gas have transformed the economy of east Scotland.

ABOVE: View over Tulloch Station east of Spean Bridge toward Stob Choire.

RIGHT: The Commando monument with Ben Nevis massif in background. Ben Nevis, the highest point in the British Isles at 4,409ft above sea level. This imposing colossus is situated close to the town of Fort William in the Lochaber area. This peak attracts over 100,000 ascents a year and not without some fatalities, mainly due to inexperience. There is, however, a relatively simple route to the summit known as the "Tourist Route" that begins at the Glen Nevis Visitor Center approximately one mile from Fort William.

FAR RIGHT: During World War II a training center for Commandos was set up at Achnacarrry Castle in the Highlands. Over 25,000 men of different nationalities —including U.S. Rangers—passed through the training and went on to contribute mightily to the war effort. This memorial stands outside Spean Bridge.

THIS PICTURE: Grampian massif from just north of Dalwhinnie.

PAGE 136: Heathland texture above Glen Truim, Dalwhinnie.

PAGE 137
ABOVE: Looking southwest over Loch Laggan, east of Spean Bridge.

BELOW: Looking northeast from the top end of Glen Shiel, near the Glenfinnan monument, over the River Shiel.

Laide burial ground on the shore of Gruinard Bay.
Gruinard Island, between Ullapool and Gairloch on
the northwest coast of Scotland, was used as a biologi-
cal warfare testing area during World War II and has
only recently been declared free of anthrax.

BELOW: Clachan Duich—the ancient church and burial ground of Clan MacRae—at the south end of Loch Duich near Kyle of Lochalsh. Note the Border Collie dog.

RIGHT: The east shore of Gruinard Bay.

Another view of Eilean Donan Castle on Loch
Duich (see also pages 110–111).

ABOVE LEFT: An abandoned farmstead in Glen Carron.

LEFT: Looking northeast over Loch Carron from near Stromeferry.

ABOVE: Looking southeast over the north end of Loch Maree, Scotland's fourth largest loch. With its wooded slopes and majestic mountain peaks surrounding it many people think it deserves the title of Scotland's prettiest loch. Loch Maree takes its name from Saint Maolrubha, the saint who crossed from Ireland to convert the Western Highlands.

RIGHT: Looking east across Gruinard Bay.

FAR RIGHT: Lily pads and reed textures on a mountain pool near Kylestrome.

BELOW: The hamlet of Ardmair on Loch Kanaird, three miles north of Ullapool. Founded as a fishing station in 1788, Ullapool's fortunes ebbed and flowed with the success of the fishing fleet,

The landscape north of Ullapool is wild and often bleak mountainside, difficult to reach by public transport and lacking the vistas of the Grampians. It possesses a wild beauty as shown in the photographs (BELOW) looking west from below the Cromalt Hills toward Ben Moir Coigach and (RIGHT) Col Beag mountain.

PAGE 150–151: Dusk light on the coast south of Scourie.

ABOVE: Burial ground of the MacLeods of Assynt at Elphin, south of Loch Assynt. The mountain to the left is Cul Mor.

LEFT: Looking southwest over the road to Ullapool from a few miles south of Elphin. The mountain on the right is Ben Mor Coigach.

PAGES 154–155: Mountain pool west near Laxford Bridge. The names of two famous racehorses figure—Foinaven, who lagged behind the leaders but won the Grand National after a multiple fall and Arkle, the horse kidnapped and killed by the IRA—can be found on maps of this area. Both are mountains east of Laxford Bridge.

THIS PICTURE: Looking southeast into Strath—meaning river valley—Dionard along the northern slopes of Foinaven.

RIGHT: The old bridge at Carrbridge near Aviemore, the main skiing resort in Scotland. Built in 1775–76, the bridge and many of the original roads in the Highlands were built by the military after the 1745 rebellion. They opened up the Highlands to government forces.

The Northern and Western Isles

FAR LEFT: The ruins of the thirteenth century church of Teampull na Trionad at Carinish, North Uist. The southern end of the Western Isles is made up of a necklace of islands and islets that over the past 60 years or so has steadily been linked together by causeways. Today it is possible to travel from Berneray and cross North Uist, Grimsay, Benbecula, and South Uist. North Uist is a stunning blend of beaches and freshwater lochs interrupted by rolling, dark moorland hills. With its Balranald nature reserve teeming with coastal waders and divers, the island is a must for bird watchers.

LEFT: The Western Isles—or Outer Hebrides—include Lewis and Harris in the north; next North Uist, Benbecula and South Uist; and then on to numerous smaller scattered isles—Eriskay, Barra, Vatersay, and others. This photograph was taken on South Uist and shows the view over Loch Druyidbeg toward Hecla. South Uist is the second largest of the Western Isles and features some remarkable sandy beaches on the Atlantic coast, while in the east the mountains of Beinn Mhor and Hecla dominate the landscape. Bridges and causeways link North and South Uist to Benbecula, the island of fords. Benbecula is the administrative center of the Southern Isles and is the most built-up area of the Outer Hebrides outside Stornoway.

BELOW LEFT: Fishing boat in the Little Minch, the waters between North Uist and Skye.

PAGE 160–161: The windswept Western Isles or Outer Hebrides is one of Scotland's most beautiful and remote areas. They are steeped in history and have been inhabited for more than 6,000 years; the spectacular Standing Stones of Calanais (Callanish) remind us of their ancient past.

THIS PICTURE: Clach (clan gathering stone) Mhicleoid standing stone near Horgabost, on Harris, looking southwest. The island was held by the Macleods from the surrender of the Norsemen in the thirteenth century until sold in 1779.

ABOVE: The prehistoric stone circle of Pobull Fhinn on the flank of Ben Langass, North Uist.

ABOVE RIGHT: Dun Carloway is an Iron Age broch on Lewis.

BELOW: Landscape west of Rueval, South Uist.

Of all the Inner Hebrides, Skye has the most in common with the Western Isles, with nearly half the population speaking Gaelic. The island is one of the most visited parts of the Highlands and has some of the most dramatic and challenging mountain terrain in Scotland.

PAGE 168–169: Interior of the restored "black house" at Colbost, Isle of Skye. The black houses—tigh dubh—were the typical dwellings of the Hebrides, with thick walls, peat rooves, and peat fires without chimneys.

RIGHT: Skye is an archaeologist's dream with geological treasures, fossils, and evidence of settlements dating back to the middle stone age, 6500 B.C. Standing stones, brochs, cairns, and monastic sites show the later inhabitants of Scots, Picts, and the Viking invasion.

FAR RIGHT: Waterfall and sea cliffs at Kilt Rock on the Trotternish Peninsula, Isle of Skye.

BELOW: Croft near Sgioport, South Uist.

THIS PICTURE: Looking west over the
Skye Bridge to Bla Bheinn from
Kyle of Lochalsh.

PAGE 174–175: The Comet Stone
and the Ring of Brodgar silhouetted
against the evening sky. The ring—
at Stenness on Mainland of the
Orkney Isles—dates from the third
millennium B.C.

Clickhimmin Broch on Mainland, Shetland
Islands, with part of the surrounding settlement
in the foreground.

Fishing & Whisky

View over the Crowlin Islands toward the
Isle of Raasay from Kyle of Lochalsh.

ABOVE: The fruits of the sea—fresh prawns. Scotland is noted for its shellfish and shrimps.

RIGHT: Limpet shells on the beach near Tarbet on Loch Fyne. Loch Fyne is a long sea loch in Argyll. From deep in the heart of the Argyll mountains it stretches firstly southwest and then southeast to open into the Sound of Bute. The scenery is magnificent throughout the whole length of the loch and it is well known for fishing and oysters. On the west side of the loch, a little inland, lies the village of Auchindrain, an old Highland hamlet that lay uninhabited for years. In 1963 a local trust started transforming it into an entire and complete museum depicting Highland life and architecture. To the south of the loch, the ruined castle that stands on the shores of East Loch Tarbert was once owned by Robert the Bruce. At the southernmost point of the loch Ardamont Point overlooks the Sound of Bute and the lovely Isle of Arran.

FAR RIGHT: Smoking trout at Inverawe. Brown trout. The River Solway and its tributaries in the southwest is famous for its sea trout as well as big late-running salmon. If one fish were to symbolize the great variety of Scottish fishing it would surely have to be the brown trout. Wild brownies are found throughout the country's many and varied waters.

RIGHT: Copper pot stills, Laphroaig Whisky Distillery, Islay. The abundance of fresh, clear water in Scotland has provided some of the best angling in the world and it has also been responsible for one of the country's most valuable exports—whisky. The unique geography and climate is ideally suited to the production of the "Water of Life." The single malts have individuality, each with their own distinctive taste in no little part due to the water source used by the distillery. The production of whisky undergoes five stages: malting, mashing, fermentation, distillation, and maturation. During the malting process the barley is steeped in bins for a few days before being spread on the malting floor where it is turned regularly to promote germination. It is spread out on a mesh platform under which a peat fire burns and the smoke is allowed to permeate the grains. Next the malted barley is milled then mixed with water in a large tank and stirred until the sugars break down to produce a sweet liquid called "wort." The wort is then transferred into lidded tanks and yeast is added to trigger fermentation and to produce a liquid called "wash." In the distillation process, the wash is cleaned up in heated stills. The stills cause their liquid contents to vaporize upward to a swan-shaped neck where condensation occurs and the spirit is drawn off. In the final process the spirit is stored in oak casks for about three years after which the product can officially be called Scotch whisky.

FAR RIGHT: Ardbeg whisky distillery, Islay. Islay malts (such as Laphroaig and Lagavulin) are peaty and intense.

The harbor at Kinlochbervie, Sutherland.

THIS PICTURE: Glengarrisdale Bay on island of Jura.

ABOVE RIGHT: Stonehaven Harbor.

BELOW RIGHT: Lybster Harbor.

PAGE 188
ABOVE: Loch angling on Loch Awe halfway between Elphin and Inchnadamph. The 24-mile-long, narrow and deep freshwater Loch Awe is the third largest loch in Scotland. It extends northeast from Ford to Kilchurn Castle near Dalmally. The loch has several islands including Inishail, which has the ruins of a convent and chapel and the remains of a Celtic graveyard, and Innis Chonell, which has the ruins of the castle of the Campbell Clan—the "Cradle of the Campbells." In the heyday of the Campbells, Loch Awe acted as a kind of natural moat for their protection. The northern shore of the loch is dominated by Ben Cruachan, which stands at 3,689ft above sea level and below which the Pass of Brander heads to the northwest and the coast.

BELOW: Another view of Clickhimmin Broch.

PAGE 189: Another small boat chugs out to fish.

LEFT: Looking northwest from Crinan toward Mull. The waters of the Inner Hebrides.

PAGE 192: Skye's impressive Cuillin Hills across Loch Scavaig